Karateka!

Sue Leather and Marje Brash

HEINEMANN ELT NEW WAVE READERS

It is 9.15 on Thursday evening. Janie Roberts, a 14 year old schoolgirl, is at her karate class. It is late and she is very tired. The class finishes at 9.30.

Karate is not easy, but Janie loves it. She started learning two years ago, and now she wears an orange belt. She goes to her karate class three times a week. Sometimes she dreams during the class. Today she is dreaming about wearing a black belt.

Janie's teacher, Pete, has got a black belt. He started learning karate ten years ago. He is a good teacher and Janie likes him very much. But today Pete is angry with her. Janie isn't thinking about her exercises.

At the end of the class, Pete talks to Janie.

'What's wrong with you tonight?' he asks. 'Are you tired?'

'A little,' Janie says.

Pete wants to help her.

'What's the problem?' he asks.

'Oh, nothing. I just want to be a black belt,' Janie says.

Pete laughs. 'Then you must work hard and stop dreaming. Goodnight, Janie.'

'Goodnight, Pete.'

At home, Janie's mother is waiting for her. Janie lives with her mother, father, and brother Richard.

Richard is 16 years old. He goes to Romsey school, the same school as Janie. He plays football in the school team. He is the best footballer in the school.

Janie goes into the kitchen. Her mother is waiting for her. She smiles at Janie.

'Hello, dear,' Mrs Roberts says. 'Did you enjoy your lesson? Come and sit down. Do you want a glass of milk?'

Mrs Roberts puts some milk on the table and opens a tin of biscuits.

Janie is happy to be home. She loves her parents very much. Her mother and father are always interested in her karate lessons.

Richard is in the kitchen too. He is finishing his homework.

'Hello, superstar,' he says. 'Have you got your black belt yet?'

Janie's face is very red. She says nothing.

Richard laughs. 'No black belt tonight?' he asks. 'Oh dear, I *am* sorry.'

'Be quiet!' Janie shouts. 'Leave me alone, you stupid boy!' And she runs out of the kitchen and goes upstairs to her bedroom.

It is late, but Janie can't sleep. She is unhappy.

'Why is Richard always so horrible to me?' she asks herself. 'My friends don't laugh at me. Mum and Dad don't laugh at me. Why does he always make jokes about karate? It isn't fair. I never make jokes about football.'

Janie thinks about Pete, her teacher. 'He's right. I must work hard. I really want a black belt.'

Janie falls asleep. She dreams about karate. Pete is giving her a black belt. Richard is clapping and cheering. He is smiling at her.

After the next karate class, Pete talks to Janie.

'There's a karate competition next week in Beeston,' he says. 'Why don't you enter?'

Janie is surprised. 'Am I good enough?' she asks. 'Do you really think I can win?'

'Why not? Anyway, it's good experience for you,' Pete says.

Janie is happy when she cycles home that night. She's going to fight in her first competition!

Janie trains very hard all week. She practises fighting with other students in her class. She knows that the competition isn't going to be easy. She must fight against green belts and blue belts.

'I must be strong,' she thinks.

Then she thinks about Richard. She remembers his jokes about karate.

'I'm going to win!' she tells herself.

The day of the competition arrives. Janie goes to Beeston with Pete. Her first fight is at three o'clock in the afternoon. Janie's fight is against a girl from Beeston. She is the same age and height as Janie. Janie talks to Pete about the girl.

'She looks good. Is this her first competition?' Janie asks.

'Don't worry about her,' Pete replies. 'Think about yourself.'

At three o'clock, Janie and the girl stand opposite each other. Janie is very nervous. Everybody is watching.

'Come on, Janie!' Pete shouts. 'You can do it!'

The fight lasts three minutes. In the first two minutes, Janie wins two points. But then she begins to feel tired. In the last minute, the girl from Beeston wins three points. She wins the fight.

Janie arrives home just before dinner. She is very tired and unhappy.

'Never mind, dear,' her mother says. 'You did your best. And it was your first competition. Anyway, your father and I are proud of you.'

Janie says nothing. Her mother knows she is unhappy.

'Is Pete pleased with you?' her mother asks.

'Yes, I think so,' Janie replies. 'He says I did well.'

Just then, Richard arrives home from his football match.

'Hello, dear,' his mother says. 'Did you win?'

'Of course we won! I scored two goals.'

Janie stands up. 'I'm going upstairs, Mum,' she says.

'What's wrong with you, karate girl?' Richard asks. 'I know. You lost!'

Janie is feeling angry and tired.

'Don't call me karate girl,' she shouts. 'I'm a karateka!'

'Karateka! Karateka!' Richard laughs.

Janie runs out of the room.

It is the first karate lesson after the competition. Janie's legs are tired and she isn't thinking about her exercises. She wants to go home. She wants to relax and watch television.

'I don't think I can ever be a black belt,' she thinks to herself.

Pete understands how she feels. But he gives Janie more exercises.

'Move your legs faster, Janie,' he shouts.

Janie is very unhappy. Why is Pete shouting at her?

At the end of the class, he walks over to her.

'I've got only one question,' he says. 'Do you really want a black belt?'

Janie says nothing.

Pete smiles. 'One competition isn't the end of the world,' he says. 'You're good, Janie. You can do it, but you've got to work!'

Janie arrives home and goes to bed. She is tired but she doesn't sleep immediately.

'Pete's right,' she thinks. 'I can do it!'

It is June and nearly the end of the school year. Janie is doing well at school. She is also doing well in her karate classes.

Today Janie and her family are preparing for a very special day. It is the school prize-giving. Parents and friends of all the school children go to the school. The headmaster gives prizes to the best pupils.

The prize-giving is an important day for Richard. This year he is leaving school. He is also 'Footballer of the Year' and he's thinking about his trophy.

'Well, I'm ready,' Richard says. 'Hurry up, everybody! The Footballer of the Year can't be late for the prize-giving!'

Janie is angry with her brother.

'The only thing you talk about is the trophy,' she says. 'The Footballer of the Year isn't so important.'

The Roberts family arrive at the school at three o'clock. The prize-giving starts at half past three. It is a lovely day. The parents and pupils are outside on the school lawn. Janie is talking to her friends. All the prizes are on a large table in the school hall.

'Janie!' Janie hears her mother calling her. 'Janie, dear, where's Richard?' Mrs Roberts asks. 'I can't see him at all. Try to find him. The prize-giving starts soon.'

Janie can't see her brother on the lawn.

'He's probably in the school hall,' she thinks, 'looking at that trophy.'

She goes into the school. As she walks into the hall, she stops.

A tall man with a knife is holding her brother. Another man is putting the school trophies into a sack.

The man with the knife sees Janie and shouts, 'Don't move, kid! We've got the boy!'

Janie looks at Richard. He can't move and he is very frightened.

'Richard, what's happening?' she asks.

'I came to look at my trophy,' Richard replies.

The man puts his hand over Richard's mouth. 'Keep quiet, you two!' he shouts.

'What can I do?' thinks Janie. 'How can I help Richard?'

The man with the knife moves closer to Janie.

'Don't try to be clever,' the man warns. He pushes Janie against the wall.

The other man is still putting trophies into the sack.

'Hurry up, Dave!' the man with the knife shouts. Then he turns and smiles at Janie.

Janie stays calm. She looks at the man with the knife. Then she moves quickly. She takes his arm and sweeps with her leg. The man falls and lets go of Richard. The knife falls to the floor.

Richard is free! He runs outside and shouts for help.

Janie picks up the knife and stands in front of the door. She points the knife at the man with the trophies. He moves back when he sees the knife and drops the trophies.

But the tall man is on his feet now and is moving towards Janie.

'Get away from me!' Janie screams.

She picks up the sack with the trophies and starts to move towards the door.

She holds the knife in one hand. The men can't get away. Janie is standing in front of the only door in the room. She feels strong and she doesn't move.

Suddenly Janie hears footsteps behind her.

'Janie!' her father shouts. 'Are you all right?'

'Quick, Dad! I've got them!' she replies.

'All right, you two,' Mr Roberts shouts. 'It's all over now.'

'Where's Richard?' Janie asks her father.

'He's phoning the police,' Mr Roberts says. 'We can hold these two until the police arrive.'

'And now the 'Footballer of the Year' trophy,' Mr Parks, the headmaster, says. 'This year the winner is Richard Roberts. Well done, Richard!'

Everyone in the hall claps. Richard looks very proud. His mother and father look proud too.

'That's the end of the school prize-giving,' says Mr Parks. 'But before we go, ladies and gentlemen, I would like to say "thank you" to a very brave young woman.'

Everyone in the hall listens. Mr Parks continues.

'Half an hour ago this young woman stopped two thieves. She saved all our trophies. Please say "thank you" to Janie Roberts.'

Janie walks onto the stage. All the parents and children are clapping and cheering. 'Well done, Janie!'

After the prize-giving, Richard runs to his sister.

'Thanks, Janie,' he says. 'You saved my trophy! I'm sorry I laughed at you before. Now I know you really are a karateka!'

Janie smiles at Richard. She is very happy. Now she knows that one day she will wear a black belt.

Macmillan Heinemann English Language Teaching, Oxford

A division of Macmillan Publishers Limited

Companies and representatives throughout the world

ISBN 0 435 27725 1

This reader is also available on cassette
ISBN 0 435 27833 9

First published 1991

Designed by Threefold Design
Illustrations by Peter Richardson

HEINEMANN ELT NEW WAVE READERS
Series Editor: Alan C. McLean
Level 2

Double Danger *by Tony Hopwood*
Karateka *by Sue Leather and Marje Brash*
Kate's Revenge *by Philip Prowse*
Zargon Zoo *by Paul Shipton*

Typeset by Threefold Design
Printed and bound in Malta by Interprint Limited

2003 2002 2001 2000 1999
13 12 11 10 9 8 7 6 5